"Sport has the power to change the world. It has the power to inspire, it has the power to unite people in a way that little else does."

—Nelson Mandela

Especially for Lynn and MicaJon, with fond memories of our backyard Olympic Games. #TeamDykes —I.L.

For Zana, Denny, Tammy, Skip, Jamie, Warren, Luci, and Trey. #FoleyAlabama —C.W.

Carolrhoda Books®
An imprint of Lerner Publishing Group, Inc.
241 First Avenue North
Minneapolis, MN 55401 USA

For reading levels and more information, look up this title at www.lernerbooks.com.

Designed by Kimberly Morales.
Main body text set in Avenir LT Pro.
Typeface provided by Linotype AG.

Library of Congress Cataloging-in-Publication Data

Names: Latham, Irene compiler | Waters, Charles, 1973– compiler
Title: For the win : poems celebrating phenomenal athletes / selected by Irene Latham and Charles Waters.
Description: Minneapolis : Carolrhoda Books, 2026. | Includes bibliographical references and index. | Audience: Ages 7–11 | Audience: Grades 2–3 | Summary: "This poetry anthology highlights twenty contemporary athletes who have overcome obstacles, broken records, and inspired the world with their athletic accomplishments" —Provided by publisher.
Identifiers: LCCN 2025018216 (print) | LCCN 2025018217 (ebook) | ISBN 9798765667996 library binding | ISBN 9798765691670 epub
Subjects: LCSH: Children's poetry, American | American poetry | CYAC: Athletes—Poetry | LCGFT: Sports poetry | Picture books
Classification: LCC PS3612.A8685 F67 2026 (print) | LCC PS3612.A8685 (ebook) | DDC 811/.6—dc23/eng/20250320

LC record available at https://lccn.loc.gov/2025018216
LC ebook record available at https://lccn.loc.gov/2025018217

Manufactured in Guang Dong, China
by Dream Colour Printing
1-1012831-53732-7/25/2025

FOR THE WIN

POEMS CELEBRATING PHENOMENAL ATHLETES

selected by
IRENE LATHAM & CHARLES WATERS

Carolrhoda Books
Minneapolis

CONTENTS

LEBRON JAMES CHANGES HIS GAME

by JaNay Brown-Wood

Toe to turf
pigskin tucked—
shuffle, swivel,
shimmy, buck.
Running back
with speed and size,
football phenom
on the rise.

Young LeBron answers the call
of an oblong, leather ball.

PAUSE . . .

Coach announces something new,
a fresh endeavor to pursue;
still needs finesse, speed, and grace—
just a different skill set to embrace.
A gift bestowed like brand-new shoes
laced up and fly,
what will he choose?

. . . PIVOT

Toe to wood
orange ball set—
hustle, dribble,
triple threat.
Power forward!
Scoring king!
Trophies, titles,
crowns, and rings.

Throughout the years, his games, his plays—
he set arenas all ablaze.
A legend on the b-ball court
among the best to play the sport!

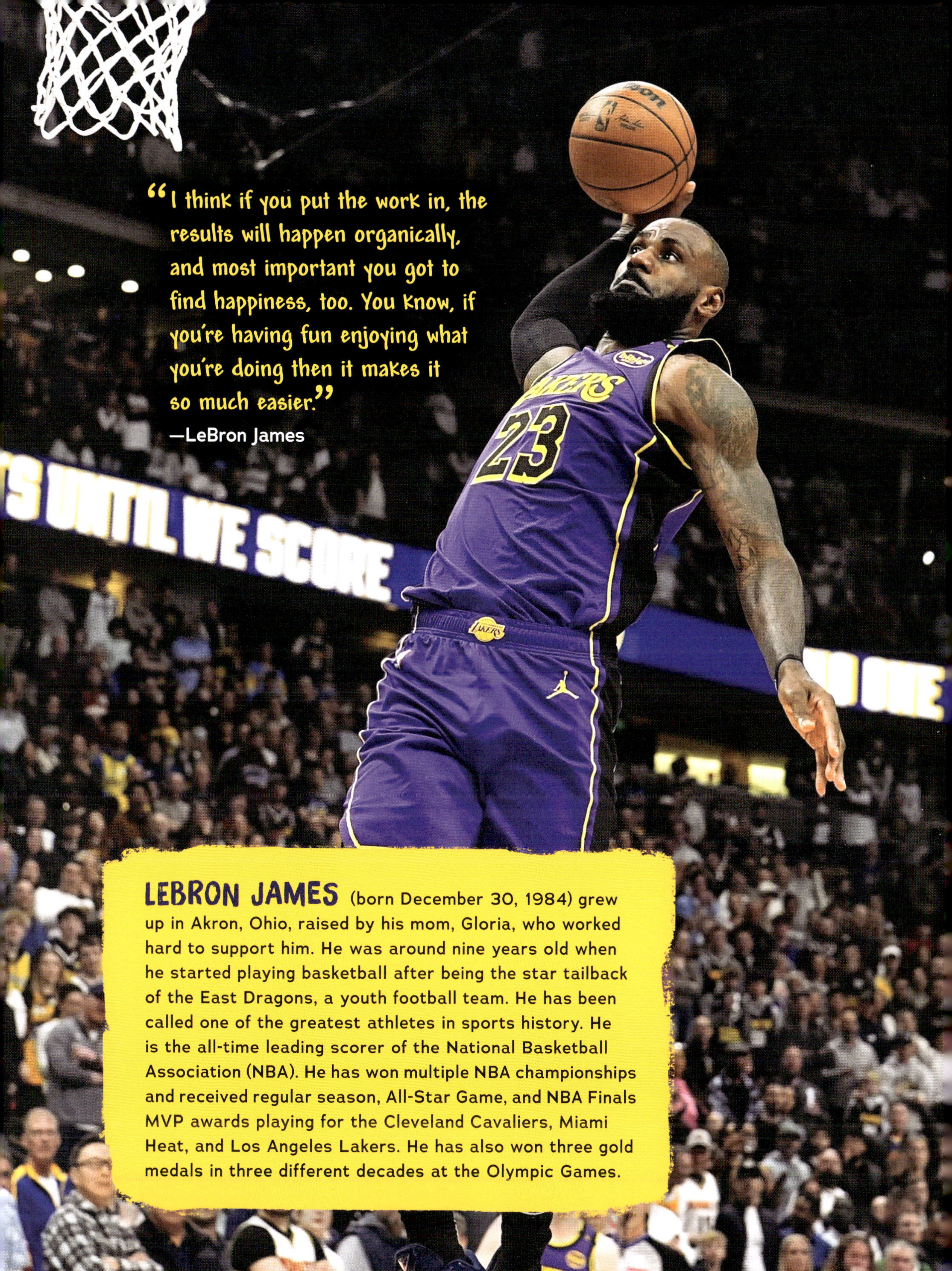

"I think if you put the work in, the results will happen organically, and most important you got to find happiness, too. You know, if you're having fun enjoying what you're doing then it makes it so much easier."

—LeBron James

LEBRON JAMES (born December 30, 1984) grew up in Akron, Ohio, raised by his mom, Gloria, who worked hard to support him. He was around nine years old when he started playing basketball after being the star tailback of the East Dragons, a youth football team. He has been called one of the greatest athletes in sports history. He is the all-time leading scorer of the National Basketball Association (NBA). He has won multiple NBA championships and received regular season, All-Star Game, and NBA Finals MVP awards playing for the Cleveland Cavaliers, Miami Heat, and Los Angeles Lakers. He has also won three gold medals in three different decades at the Olympic Games.

SOPHIA WILSON'S RECIPE FOR SOCCER SUCCESS

by Laura Shovan and Leah Henderson

Gather two cups of confidence
and a quart of creativity.
Grab a handful of grit
and a pound of passionate work ethic.
Spin together with
  speed balance coordination.

Mix belief in yourself
with parents
who pick you up early from school
and drive three hours
round trip, so you can
  practice and practice and practice.

Add a dash of dinner in the back seat
and a huge helping of homework
on the ride home.
Fold in caring coaches who see
how good you could be, as you
  drill and drill and drill.

Cut out negative voices,
then dress the mixture
with ball control, finesse,
quick turns,
and one-on-one dominance,
  dribble and dribble and dribble.

One last step before serving to an athlete
with a willingness to learn
and a heaping love for the game,
sprinkle with a special ingredient—
a talent for scoring
  goal after goal after goal.

"My parents sacrificed so much for me to be able to play this game. They knew I had a dream and did everything they could to help me reach it."
—Sophia Wilson

SOPHIA WILSON (born August 10, 2000) is an American professional soccer player originally from Colorado. She went by the name of Sophia Smith until her 2025 marriage to National Football League (NFL) player Michael Wilson. Sophia fell in love with soccer at an early age. In high school she was chosen as the 2017 US Soccer Young Player of the Year. She played two seasons at Stanford University, where her team won the 2019 National Collegiate Athletic Association (NCAA) Championship. In 2022 she led the US Women's National Soccer Team in goals, scoring 11 times in 17 appearances. That year she became the first woman of color to be named US Female Soccer Athlete of the Year. She made her World Cup debut in 2023 and won an Olympic gold medal in 2024.

KEENAN ALLEN, LUMBEE STRONG

by Kim Rogers

Storm after storm,
Keenan's ancestors see
the pain in his eyes
as he endures harsh winds.

BAM! Broken collarbone.

But "Lumbee" is inked on his left arm,
a permanent reminder of his deep roots.
His people are with him always—

CRASH! Kidney injury.

Especially his grandfather
who watched hours and hours
of NASCAR and football
with him when he was a kid.
He loves watching Keenan
play on the gridiron on TV.

WHAM! Torn ACL.

His people are with him
at every game,
rumbling with the crowd
like a thunderbird hovering overhead,
protecting and sounding off.

BOOM! 2017 NFL Comeback Player of the Year.

They knew
he would stand tall again.
And he does
like an oak tree,
resilient and strong,
a Lumbee.

"It's life . . . it's about . . . being able to go through those ups and downs and not fall out of your element, not lose yourself."
—Keenan Allen

KEENAN ALLEN (born April 27, 1992) is an American football player and a citizen of the Lumbee Tribe of North Carolina. In high school he played football and basketball and ran track. He was drafted into the NFL in 2013 by the San Diego Chargers (which later relocated to Los Angeles), and as a wide receiver, he experienced a string of injuries. In the first game of the 2016 season, he tore his anterior cruciate ligament (ACL) and was unable to play for the rest of the season. The following season, he gained the second-most receiving yards in Chargers history and made the most catches in franchise history. For those accomplishments, he was named 2017 NFL Comeback Player of the Year.

RONALD ACUÑA JR. DREAMS OF A RINGING SINGLE

by René Saldaña Jr.

"Thinking back on that time . . . it was magical."
—Ronald Acuña Jr.

Upright at the plate, La Bestia waits for the pitch, **thinking**
back to his early days of playing beísbol. His memory takes him **back**
to when he was nothing but a stick of a boy in La Sabana, taking cuts **on**
day-old newspapers crumpled into balls. **That**
kid kept at it, kept playing, biding his **time**.

Today it happened, su primer hit as a beísbolero. Patient at the plate, **it**
was just like he was back in La Sabana. The ball flew at him fast. His swing **was**
true, though, the <CRACK> sending it back up the middle, the day **magical**.

RONALD ACUÑA JR. (born December 18, 1997) grew up playing baseball in Venezuela. He has a long family connection to the sport. His younger brother and four of his cousins have all spent time playing in the major leagues. His father and grandfather were former minor league players. His father, Ronald Acuña Sr., instilled in him the motivation to run hard, lift weights, and have a good attitude so he could avoid some of the mistakes he had made as a youth. An outfielder for the Atlanta Braves, he's won both Rookie of the Year and most valuable player (MVP) honors. He made Major League Baseball (MLB) history as the only player to hit at least 40 home runs and steal at least 70 bases in a single season, also now known as the 40/70 club.

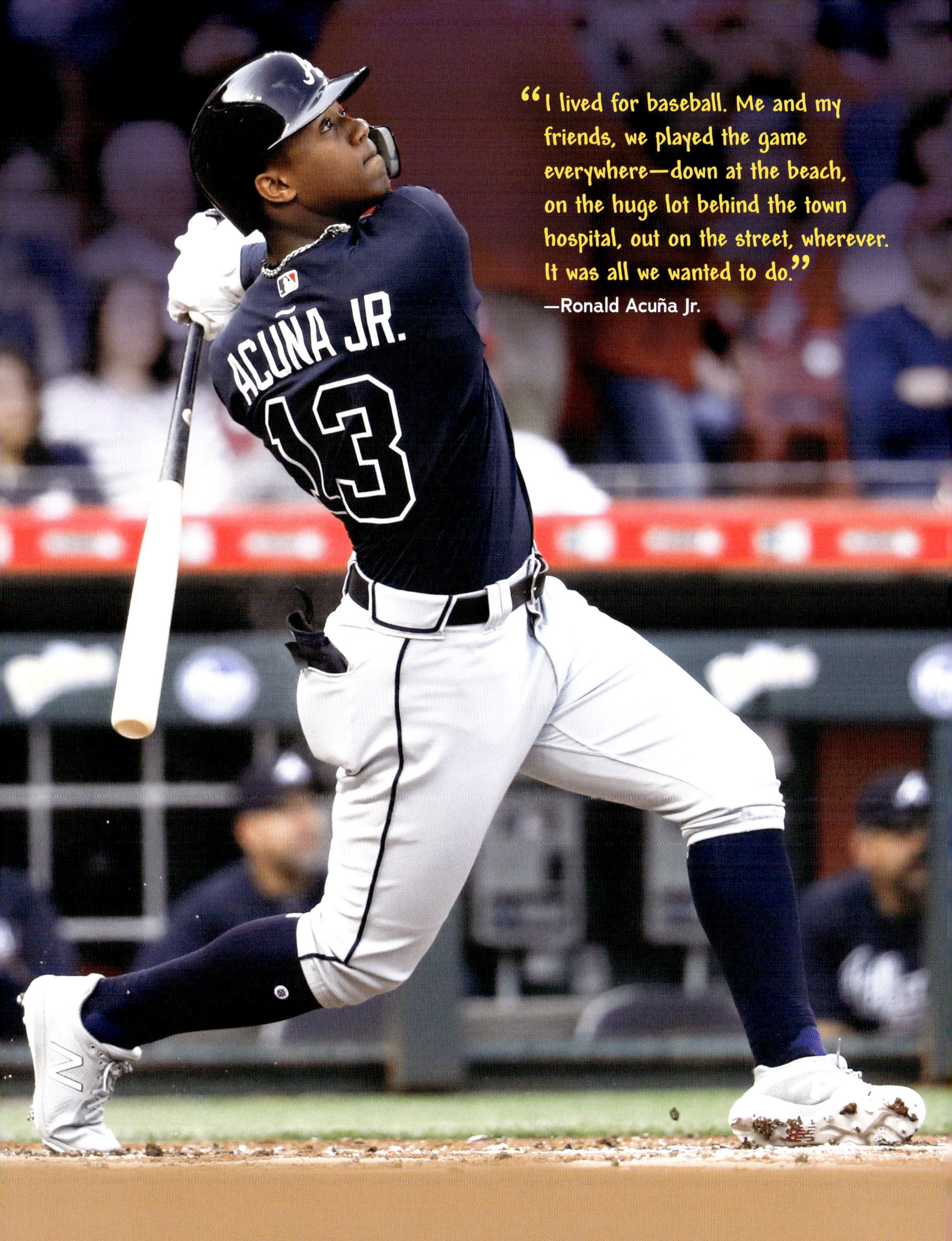

> “I lived for baseball. Me and my friends, we played the game everywhere—down at the beach, on the huge lot behind the town hospital, out on the street, wherever. It was all we wanted to do.”
>
> —Ronald Acuña Jr.

WHEN SUNI LEE COMES ON TV

by Kao Kalia Yang

When Suni Lee comes on TV,
Mother's eyes shine.
When Suni Lee comes on TV,
Grandmother's mouth opens wide.

Suni Lee stands on the floor,
Her hands are wings at her sides.
She leaps, flips, and flies,
Her outfit sparkles beneath the lights.
There's a Hmong girl shining bright.

When Suni Lee comes on TV,
a Hmong kid learning to walk, runs.
When Suni Lee comes on TV,
a Hmong kid flying off the swing lands, and bows.
They are preparing for the Olympics of the future.

When Suni Lee comes on TV,
the Hmong families on the East Side of St. Paul know:
dragons are invisible unless you know where to look.

I watch Mother and Grandmother
move in the shadows of our house.
Across the light in the yard,
to the garden that awaits,
where green things grow.
they bend,
they stand,
dragon women, who feed the future.

The gold circle dangles from Suni Lee's neck,
her chest rises and falls,
she catches her breath,
fire without flames.

SUNISA (SUNI) LEE (born March 9, 2003) grew up in St. Paul, Minnesota. She was such a tumbling ball of energy growing up that her father created a balance beam for her behind their home. Her formal training in gymnastics began at six years old. In 2021, Suni became the first Hmong American Olympian, winning a gold medal in the individual all-around, a silver medal in the team event, and a bronze medal on the uneven bars in Tokyo, Japan. At the 2024 Olympic Games in Paris, France, Suni again won gold, this time in the team event, as well as bronze medals in the individual all-around and the uneven bars.

JALEN HURTS AT THE 2018 NATIONAL CHAMPIONSHIP GAME

by Charles Waters

It hurts
to see Jalen on the sidelines.
Football competition courses through
him and his close-knit family's bloodstream
like fuel through a 12-cylinder,
twin-turbo engine.

He usually throws pinpoint lasers
or jukes the defense into human knots,
but at the national championship game,
his skill was put to the test.

First half sputtered along, missed throws,
little matriculation downfield, playing like
his turbochargers might've malfunctioned.

Jalen had lost only twice in two years,
But at halftime Coach makes the call:
the backup quarterback would take over.
Jalen's spirit threatens to short-circuit.

Instead of veering into self-pity,
potentially pulling down the team with
negativity, he faces his circumstances with dignity.
His parents, Averion Sr. and Pamela, would expect
nothing less from their middle child.

In the second half, he cheers on his team,
running in celebration as they achieve victory.

When he has a chance to get back
onto the field next year,
Jalen will be ready to lead his squad
once more.

He's so good,
it hurts.

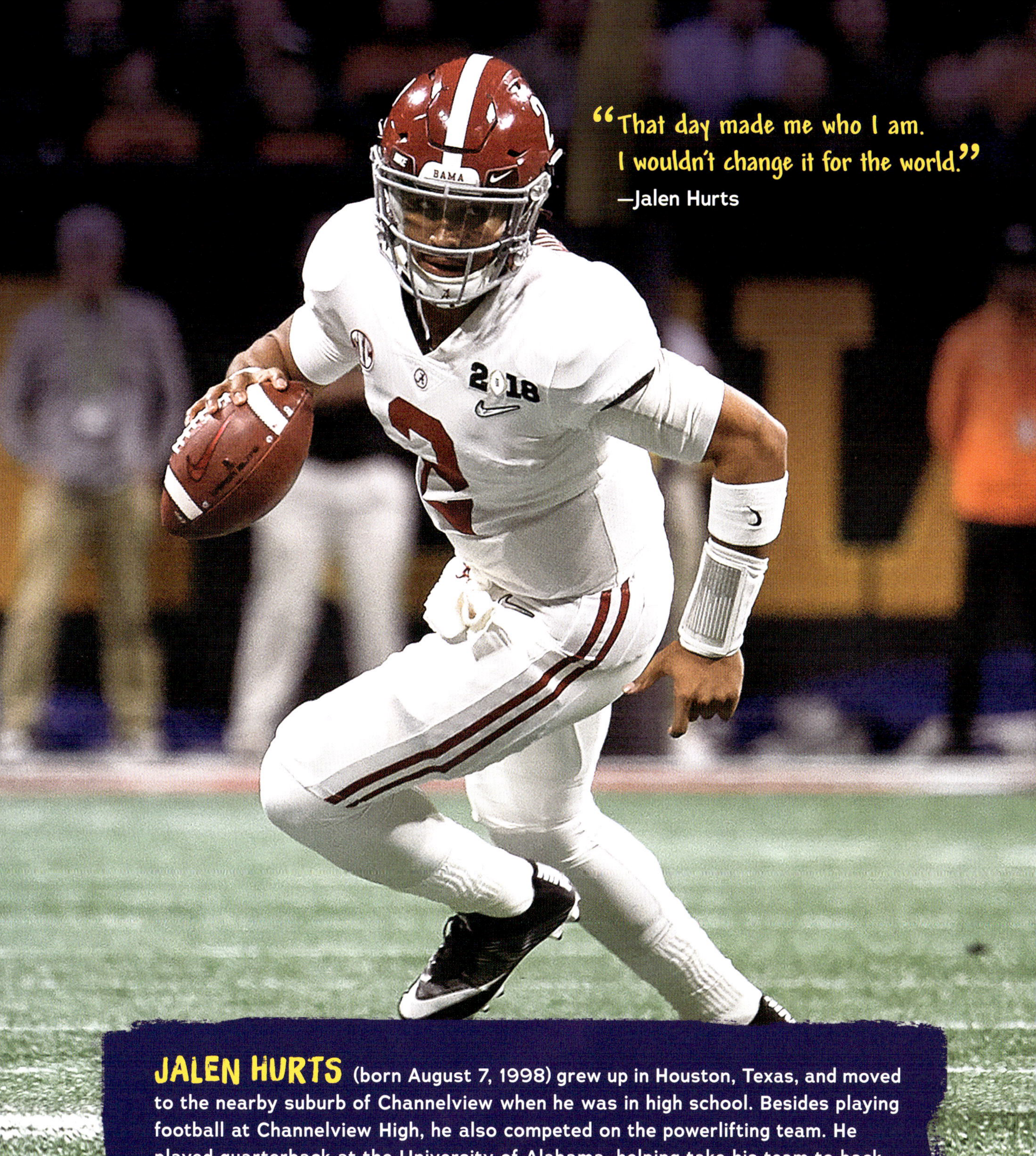

“That day made me who I am. I wouldn’t change it for the world.”
—Jalen Hurts

JALEN HURTS (born August 7, 1998) grew up in Houston, Texas, and moved to the nearby suburb of Channelview when he was in high school. Besides playing football at Channelview High, he also competed on the powerlifting team. He played quarterback at the University of Alabama, helping take his team to back-to-back national championship games. After his third season, he transferred to the University of Oklahoma, where he finished in second place for the Heisman Trophy. In 2020, he was drafted into the NFL by the Philadelphia Eagles. Almost five years later, he led the Eagles to a Super Bowl victory over the Kansas City Chiefs and was named Super Bowl MVP.

NAOMI OSAKA TAKES A BREATH

by Anita Yasuda

She is more
than today's Paris match.
Serve, swing—slice
More than four Grand Slams
and one clay court.

She is more
than chasing
racing after titles,
because she's willing
to say, *no more*.

From stands, fan-thunder
pounds down.
More press, publicity,
and pressure?
Please . . . STOP!

She needs a break.
Time to pause, rest;
away from the top.
Time to embrace small to-YAYS
and not O-kays.

More seasons spent
breathing—
s l o w.
Seeing worries unfold
and go.

Beautiful
blue
sky soothes.
Now she is breathless
no more.

NAOMI OSAKA (born October 16, 1997) is originally from Osaka, Japan. Her father is Haitian, and her mother is Japanese. They moved to Elmont, New York, when she was preschool age. Naomi started playing tennis at three years old. At the US Open—one of the four major tennis tournaments—in 2018, she became the first Japanese player to win a Grand Slam event. She has also won multiple Grand Slam tournaments since then and has represented Japan in the Olympics. During her career, Naomi has struggled with depression, and she withdrew from the 2021 French Open to get a break from the intense pressure and take more time for her mental health. She has continued to play professionally while also building a life outside of the sport, including speaking out on social justice issues and, in 2023, becoming a mom.

"I do hope that people can relate and understand it's O.K. to not be O.K., and it's O.K. to talk about it. There are people who can help, and there is usually light at the end of any tunnel."

—Naomi Osaka

JUAN SOTO AND HIS WORLD SERIES BIRTHDAY

by Guadalupe Garcia McCall

In the Dominican Republic,
Juan Jose Soto's father
celebrates his tenth birthday

with the wonder and whirl
of the 2008 World Series
roaring in the background.

In a moment of joy, his father
tells Juan Soto, "Listen, one
day you'll be in the World

Series. You will be there."
Excited, Juan Soto takes time off
video games and begins playing

baseball in Herrera, their barrio on
the west side of Santo Domingo.
Sometimes, he sends baseballs

soaring up, up, up high into
the sky toward a smiling sun.
His father predicts Juan Soto

will someday spend his birthday
with crowds of people cheering
him on at a World Series game.

And so it happens, with hard
work and dedication, Juan Soto
becomes a star in the major

leagues, entertaining his fans
with his famous Soto Shuffle
every time he's up to bat.

On an October night, while
his father watches from the stands,
Juan Soto makes history with a

left-center field home run, just
days before his twenty-first birthday.
The world will never forget Juan Soto,

that win, or the Soto Shuffle.

"We were watching a World Series game, and he told me, 'One day, hey, you're going to be playing in the World Series on your birthday. One day, you will see.' And now, the dream is coming true, and it just feels amazing."

—Juan Soto

JUAN SOTO (born October 25, 1998) is a baseball player from Santo Domingo, Dominican Republic. As a child, he would use a bottle in place of a bat and hit balled-up pieces of paper and bottle caps thrown by his father to develop his extraordinary hand-eye coordination. It worked—Juan became an MLB star with the Washington Nationals and helped them win the World Series in 2019. He also became the fourth-youngest player to hit a home run in a World Series, the second youngest to hit one in their first World Series game, and—in Game 3—the youngest to play on his birthday. Juan has been named to multiple All-Star teams and is known not only for his incredible hitting skills but also his playful attitude on the field.

THE OILERS' CAPTAIN'S "C" CONSIDERS CONNOR McDAVID'S CAPTAINCY

by Jay Brazeau

C is for craftily cradling the puck.
C is for
> CRACK <
of the shot when it's struck.
C is for carving his way through the zone.

C means I'm carefully measured and sewn.

C is for crowds who believed what he'd be.
C is for cast as The Next One—
we'll see, because
C is for caution!
He's only 19—
he's not The Great One
(you know who I mean).

C means created for this solemn space.
C is how calmly he takes his place.
C is his confidence in what lies ahead—
and hope—a wish in each stitch of my thread.

C is for chest, where I'm set in position.
C is for chosen—a *historic* decision, because
C is for Connor, the youngest to don
me—
the C.

We're ready. *GAME ON!!*

CONNOR MCDAVID (born January 13, 1997) hails from Richmond Hills, Ontario, Canada. He was rollerblading successfully when he was just shy of three years old. When he was four, he was playing organized hockey. Connor has accomplished a variety of firsts in his career: the youngest player named captain for his team, the Edmonton Oilers, and the youngest to be the leading scorer in the National Hockey League (NHL). He's also won multiple Hart Memorial Trophies as the league's most valuable player.

A'JA WILSON'S SIDELINE SECRET

by Lacresha Berry

A'ja Wilson, a dominator of the paint.
a dynamic defensive motor
    grabbing rebounds
    making fadeaways
nearly no faults
in her game.
a superstar forward
now known by her first name.

but, at fifteen
when the specialist
pulled her from her English class,
A'ja Wilson heard no cheers
from the stands and
no championship chants.
just a specialist passing
her paragraphs to decipher,
the words bouncing up and down,
    dribbling across the page
    too fast for her
to keep the phrases
in bounds.

You have dyslexia,
the specialist said.

A'ja's heart dropped,
her shot clock stopped.
no matter the diagnosis,
she's not giving up
on her basketball dreams.

carrying
her sideline secret
until her second year
at South Carolina.
figuring no one needs to know
(except Coach).

so now, off the court she conquers
the hard press on the page.
learning to take it slow
as she decodes words and phrases.
to go and grow at her own pace—

to glow.

“You have to go at your own pace.”
—A’ja Wilson

A’JA WILSON (born August 8, 1996) grew up in Hopkins, South Carolina. As a high school senior, she was named a McDonald’s All-American and led her team to a state title. In 2017 she led her University of South Carolina team to a national championship. She was the first overall pick in the 2018 Women’s National Basketball Association (WNBA) Draft and has since become a standout player for the Las Vegas Aces, winning MVP awards and helping her team win championships. She also led the US women’s basketball team to a gold medal at the 2024 Olympics. In 2019 A’ja and her parents founded the A’ja Wilson Foundation to help children struggling with dyslexia and bullying.

WATER WELCOMES JESSICA LONG

by Sarah Grace Tuttle

Kneel on the starting block.

Brace yourself
for the challenge to come.
When you dive in,
Water welcomes you
to find your pace.

Splash!

When you dive in,
go! Swim as hard as you can.
Water will not tire.
Water welcomes you
to test yourself.

Nubs kick, arms pull, pull, pull . . .

Water will not tire,
so force your aching body forward.
Swim despite your doubts.
Water welcomes you
to defy yourself.

Pull . . . stretch . . . touch the wall!

Swim despite your doubts.

Catch your breath after conquering
    one-hundred-and-twenty-eight
    laborious
    laps.
Water welcomes you
to celebrate your strength.

JESSICA LONG (born February 29, 1992) is originally from Bratsk, Russia. Shortly after she turned one year old, she was adopted and moved to Baltimore, Maryland. Jessica was born with fibular hemimelia, missing most of the bones in her lower legs and feet. She was fitted with prosthetics when she was a year and half after the amputation of her lower legs. She started swimming in her grandmother's pool, and by the age of ten, she was defeating nondisabled swimmers in races. She became the youngest member of the US Paralympic Team at twelve years old and went on to win three gold medals in the 2004 Paralympic Games. Since then she has added heavily to her totals.

“I’m not just determined in swimming. I’m determined in everything that I do.”
—Jessica Long
arena

NELLY KORDA TAKES A DAY OFF

by Irene Latham

After endless mornings
hitting the gym

a thousand practice rounds,
ten thousand buckets of balls

dialing in on the shot
        the swing
        the follow-through—

Finally, Nelly takes a recovery day
with her sister Jess.

They trade golf cleats
for fluffy slippers,
share news & memories:
        remember when we were kids
        & we both won our divisions the same day?

Nelly—always training—
confesses dreams & struggles,
fears & strategies:
        check alignment
        adjust stance;
        if you're going to curve it, you have to control it.

The world shrinks
to the size of the pizza they're sharing—

a slice of forever,
a pie to nourish & sustain Nelly
for now

for the next tournament
& for every next hole.

"Life gets pretty lonely out here, traveling destination to destination. So it's fun to have someone in the same hotel and have automatic practice rounds together, too . . . and it definitely makes life a lot easier."

—Nelly Korda

NELLY KORDA (born July 28, 1998) started playing golf consistently when she was six years old, practicing multiple times a week. She is also the youngest child in a family of athletes: both of her parents, Petr and Regina, were professional tennis players; brother Sebastian is also a professional tennis player; and sister Jessica retired from the Ladies Professional Golf Association (LPGA) Tour in 2023. An Olympic gold medalist, Nelly currently plays on the LPGA Tour. She has also been ranked number one in the Women's World Golf Rankings, winning multiple major championships along the way. She and Jessica refer to themselves as "built-in best buddies."

APRAR HASSAN'S JOURNEY TO KARATE GOLD

by Naaz Khan

Sandan on. Ready to go,
but then . . . an unexpected, "No."
Hijab not allowed? Disqualification?
But what is the referee's justification?

Coaches, contestants, and strangers unite.
Encourage Aprar, "They must let you fight!"
Our champion karate star must decide!
Accept and silently step aside?
Or make a tough, courageous choice?
Share her knowledge? Use her voice?

Loud and proud, conversations begin
about a recent policy win:
the stance of the World Karate Federation
and rights to religious modification.
Official statement and solid support
for the "integration power" of the sport.

Soon Aprar is let back on the floor,
but the moment's distraction is hard to ignore . . .

One week later. At nationals now.
Hajime! Start! Aprar takes a bow.

Yoi. Attention. In starting position.
Swiftly, she punches, with strength and precision.
Ki-ai! Energy-focus! She yells.
Tsuki! Punch! *Keri*. Kick! Our champ excels!
Oi zuki! Front punch! Precise, strong, and quick!
Mawashi-geri! Roundhouse kick!
With power, speed, technique, motivation
She fights each round with deep concentration
At last, *sanbon kumite*—three step spar!
She goes in for the win . . . and its gold for Aprar!

“If someone says no, and is being unfair, speak up! Stand up! Fight for your dreams. Sometimes difficult moments are opportunities to become stronger.”
—Aprar Hassan

APRAR HASSAN (born August 9, 2002) is an Egyptian American karate champion from Brooklyn, New York. Following in the footsteps of her father, Yasser Salama, who was a member of the Egyptian national karate team, Aprar began competing as a young child. Since turning professional as a teenager, she has racked up many championships. She is the first Muslim woman to become a part of the Amateur Athletic Union’s USA National Karate Team. She has faced and overcome obstacles such as almost being disqualified at different times for wearing her hijab and a white turtleneck under her karate attire. In addition to competing, she has become a world-ranked referee and an Amateur Athletic Union Ambassador.

HOW EILEEN GU NAVIGATES THE SKY

by Nancy Tupper Ling

With each jump and jib,
    mogul and turn
down Lake Tahoe's slopes,
    young Eileen Gu 谷爱凌
uncovers her North Star.

By eight, she enrolls in freeski;
    "racing" seems too dangerous
to her mother, Yan Gu.
    Turns out this stunt-style school
feels anything but safe.

How Eileen loves the rush,
    the launch and release
upward, into snow-filled clouds.
    Soon she conquers
aerials and corks,

vertical axis rotations,
    and ambidextrous spins,
Before every run
    she faces her fears.

Eyes closed,
    she envisions her body in flight,
each rotation, each perfect landing.
    She breathes deep,

captures the dreaded flutters
    inside her chest,
then catapults down the slope.

Eileen navigates each new terrain,
    her mother beside her
like a team.
    Still, when Eileen paints the sky
with her freestyle moves—

Half-pipe, slopestyle
    big air Olympic wins—
Yan Gu always looks away
    until her daughter touches down gracefully,
like a red-crowned crane from a snowy sky.

"Achieving the impossible has always been something that has drawn me in."

—Eileen Gu

EILEEN GU (born September 3, 2003) hails from San Francisco, California. Her skiing journey began at the age of three when her mother, Yan, a former investment banker and ski instructor, introduced Eileen to the slopes. At nine Eileen won a national championship. Since then she has won a variety of medals at both the Winter X Games and the FIS Freestyle World Ski Championships. During the 2022 Olympics in Beijing, China, eighteen-year-old Eileen represented her mother's home country of China, winning two gold medals and one silver medal. Accomplishing this feat made Eileen the youngest freestyle skiing Olympic champion in history.

COCO GAUFF'S FULL CIRCLE FIRE

by Glenis Redmond

By age eight, Coco
puts a match to kindling
on the court,
and on the steps
of Arthur Ashe Stadium,
as she does a happy-go-lucky dance
to "Call Me Maybe" between sets
watching Serena Williams win the US Open.
It's as if Coco and Serena's fingertips touch
and starfire is passed.
Behold Black Girl Magic!
The spark that burns
as she trains and trains.
Some say, *What's all the racket?*
Don't worry; Coco silences them
with the trajectory of her swing.
Look up. See a little Black girl
turn into a young Black woman
shooting into the stratosphere.
As she grand slams with grace,
watch her take the heat of hate,
return it with her two-handed backhand,
and win the US Open.
She schools doubters—
it's not water they pour
onto her dreams, but gasoline.
Watch her make history
as she blossoms
into a blaze.

CORI “COCO” GAUFF (born March 13, 2004) spent her early years in Atlanta, Georgia, and when she was seven years old, her family moved to Delray Beach, Florida, so she could focus on tennis. She made history in 2023 when she became the youngest American woman since Serena Williams to win the US Open. She faced backlash from some fans who felt she was overhyped. Instead of feeling defeated, Coco used this as inspiration. An activist on and off the court, Coco has used her influence to speak out on inequality, depression, and climate change issues. She has also helped fund new tennis courts and a playground in Georgia.

THE RISE OF ROMAN REIGNS

by Edna Cabcabin Moran

Before he was Roman,
he was Joe.

Football-obsessed kid from Pensacola
in line with his teammates,
a shroud of padding topped with a helmet—

a clone
like the others.

But Joe
is son of Sika
and nephew of Afa
from the WWE Hall of Famers team,
the Wild Samoans.

Family matters.

He ditches his cleats,
leaves for the ring.

Inked lines
carry tribal symbols
baring skin-deep stories.
Little is hidden,
which takes getting used to.

Joe flexes and preens
poses for half a beat (feels like half a lifetime).

He pounces on the opponent,
lurches into chaos:
bodies colliding, careening,
swerving in and out of reach.

Proclaims himself
Tribal Chief—

better to be the tough guy
heel
than baby face
good guy

on repeat
on full display.
He is ROMAN REIGNS!

The Bloodline
pulses on.

"I feel like I've always been in that position in my family, to raise the bar, to keep our legacy strong."
—Roman Reigns

ROMAN REIGNS (born May 25, 1985), whose given name is Leati Joseph Anoa'i, is the third generation of the legendary Anoa'i family wrestling dynasty. He was born and raised in Pensacola, Florida, and in high school he was named Defensive Player of the Year by the *Pensacola News Journal* for his football exploits. In college he was a first-team All-Atlantic Coast Conference (ACC) defensive tackle for the Georgia Tech Yellow Jackets. After college he played in the Canadian Football League for a brief stint before retiring from football in 2008. As a professional wrestler for World Wrestling Entertainment (WWE), Roman also goes by the name Tribal Chief and has won a variety of championship belts.

MOOKIE BETTS PLAYS CATCH WITH THE PAST

by Jaime Adoff

The arc of the ball is long . . .
bending toward the plate
and that just reward
for a batter who waits
for his pitch.
The crack of Mookie's bat
L
A
U
N
C
h
e
s

the ball—into an idea
A vision of the future

from the past

traveling fast

into Jackie's glove

where he turned

hate into LOVE

Bringing **Power**
To His People

Jackie Robinson reaches down
to touch that hallowed Dodger ground
He brushes off
that sweet Brooklyn dust
and throws the ball back to

Mookie Betts
Now playing catch with the past
to AFFECT *CHANGE*
"Well ahead of the game"
Mookie stands as tall as the shadows that
came before him
Those who broke down walls
so he could watch the long arc of the ball
bend toward that center field fence
and land in the hands of that young fan
who will soon understand
there is more to life
than

balls and strikes.

“I don’t want to be just the athlete . . .
I know I’m more than that.”
—Mookie Betts

MARKUS “MOOKIE” BETTS (born October 7, 1992) is from Nashville, Tennessee. Due to his smaller stature as a youth, he wasn’t taken seriously by Little League coaches. This led his mother, Diana, to create her own baseball team so Mookie could play. He has been a part of a number of World Series championship teams, selected to play in various All-Star games, won multiple Gold Gloves as the best right fielder, and has been voted Most Valuable Player. Off the field, Mookie helped put together the documentary *Jackie Robinson: Get to the Bag*. This film explores the life and times of his fellow Dodger, Jackie Robinson, who was arguably one of the most consequential figures in history—on April 15, 1947, Jackie became the first Black player to play in the major leagues since Moses Fleetwood Walker in 1884.

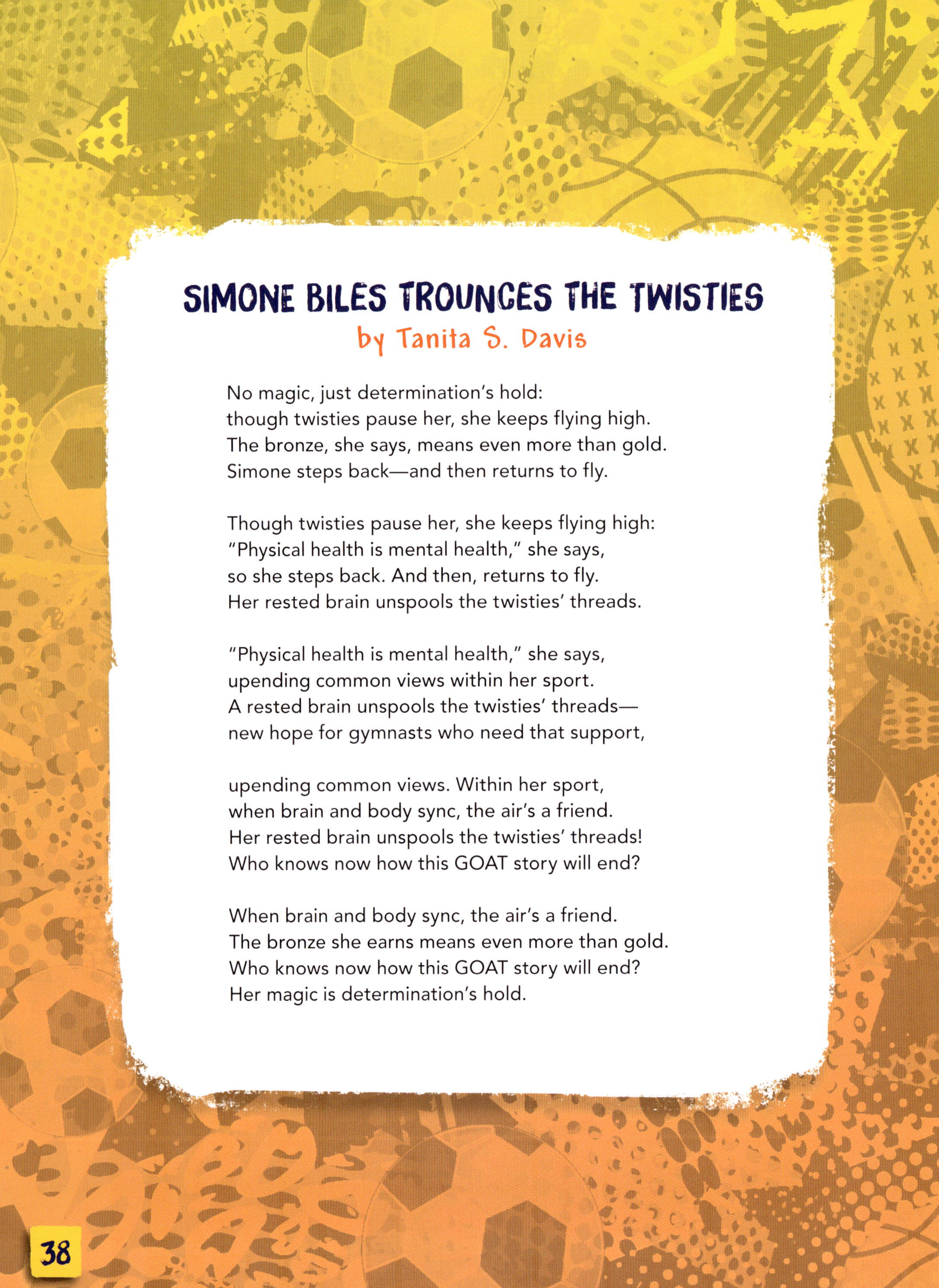

SIMONE BILES TROUNCES THE TWISTIES

by Tanita S. Davis

No magic, just determination's hold:
though twisties pause her, she keeps flying high.
The bronze, she says, means even more than gold.
Simone steps back—and then returns to fly.

Though twisties pause her, she keeps flying high:
"Physical health is mental health," she says,
so she steps back. And then, returns to fly.
Her rested brain unspools the twisties' threads.

"Physical health is mental health," she says,
upending common views within her sport.
A rested brain unspools the twisties' threads—
new hope for gymnasts who need that support,

upending common views. Within her sport,
when brain and body sync, the air's a friend.
Her rested brain unspools the twisties' threads!
Who knows now how this GOAT story will end?

When brain and body sync, the air's a friend.
The bronze she earns means even more than gold.
Who knows now how this GOAT story will end?
Her magic is determination's hold.

“[The bronze] means more than all the golds because I’ve been through so much.”

—Simone Biles

SIMONE BILES (born March 14, 1997) is originally from Columbus, Ohio, and moved to Spring, Texas, a suburb of Houston, where she was adopted by her grandparents. At six years old Simone went on a field trip to a gymnastics center and became interested in the sport. She has won the most medals in the sport’s history and the most Olympic medals by a gymnast. Simone was also the first to land several moves in competition, which are now named after her. She temporarily withdrew from the Tokyo Olympics in 2021 due to the twisties—getting disoriented while twisting in the air—before returning to competition and winning a bronze medal in the women’s balance beam. In three Olympics—Rio de Janeiro, Brazil; Tokyo; and Paris—she has won a total of eleven medals (seven gold, two silver, and two bronze).

LIONEL MESSI REACHES FOR MORE

by Mariana Dominé

A small boy from Rosario
looked at the stars in the night sky—
reached for one of them.

One day, he would bring one home,
wear it proudly on his chest.

Un día,
he would become one of them.

La pulga, they called him, for the way he moved,
a speed so fast, he left opponents in his stardust.

Lionel Messi's dream glistened
just beyond his grasp, gained distance
as his peers stretched taller around him.

When his growth condition was discovered,
his childhood team chose to believe in his potential—
funded the medicine he needed to reach his light.

Now, our captain reaches for more,
mapping out plays
on
and off
the field—strings
of passes, like constellations
being formed before his eyes.

He sees his past in the eyes
of the children he helps with his foundation,
stars waiting to launch
with support from their team.

Somewhere, another child
looks at the stars in the night sky—
reaches for one of them.

“Being a bit famous now gives me the opportunity to help people who really need it, particularly children.”

—Lionel Messi

LIONEL MESSI (born June 24, 1987) is a world-famous soccer player from Rosario, Argentina. His dreams might have been derailed if his team hadn't helped pay for the medicine to treat a growth hormone deficiency. As a teenager, he joined Futbol Club (FC) Barcelona, a professional soccer team based in Spain, where he won many championships and awards. He was also a key member of Argentina's national team, particularly notable in the team's 2022 World Cup victory. He joined Major League Soccer (MLS) team Inter Miami in 2023 and is known for his charitable efforts. Through his Leo Messi Foundation, he supports children around the world by building schools, providing medical care, and offering sports programs, most often in Argentina and Spain.

PATRICK MAHOMES CREATES HIS LEGACY

by Darius Phelps

Whether on the field
or at a press conference

time passes quicker
than anything

his two hands
can grasp.

No matter how much
things change . . .

No matter how much
his success brings fame . . .

for him, there will always be
things that remain the same.

Faith.
Family.
Love.

Beneath the soles of his cleats
lies a foundation none can mistake—

A mother's love may light the path,
but it's his footsteps that leave the imprint.

Watch as he scrambles—eyes scanning,
body twisting midair, defying physics and doubt.

This is the Mahomes Effect:
success born from chaos,

throws no one else would dare attempt—
a symphony of instinct and improvisation.

In the noise, he finds clarity.
In the pressure, he finds poetry.

He doesn't just play the game—
he redefines it, one no-look pass at a time.

TOUCHDOWN!

“I want to be the best family man, football player, businessman I can be and hopefully make a great impact in this world.”
—Patrick Mahomes

PATRICK MAHOMES (born September 17, 1995) starred in three sports (baseball, basketball, and football) at Whitehouse High School in Texas. During his college years at Texas Tech, he decided to focus on football, and he's never looked back. As a quarterback for the Kansas City Chiefs, he has won not only multiple Super Bowls but multiple Super Bowl MVPs as well. His accomplishments include NFL MVP Awards, Associated Press (AP) First-Team All-Pro honors, and being named the *Sports Illustrated* Sportsperson of the Year. Patrick's spontaneous, freewheeling style of play has influenced a generation of quarterbacks in what is called the Mahomes Effect.

ABOUT THE POETS

JAIME ADOFF grew up watching the legendary Cincinnati Reds of the 1970s, nicknamed the Big Red Machine, developing his love for baseball and his ability to sneak down from the nosebleed seats to those just behind the dugout! Jaime is an award-winning young adult author and children's poet. His most recent picture books are *Violet and the Frost King* and *Rock n Roll Dad*. www.therealjaimeadoff.com

LACRESHA BERRY was raised in Kentucky with the love of basketball in her blood. This passion led her to play on her middle school basketball team and in after-school pickup games with her older brothers. Even though she later stopped playing, her love for the sport continued, and she loves following the WNBA and A'ja Wilson. www.berryandconyc.com

JAY BRAZEAU is a poet from Ottawa, Canada. His poems have appeared in anthologies, print and online magazines, and public art projects. As a young hockey player, Jay was named captain of the Riverside Park Atom House League "B" Islanders during their 1982–1983 championship-winning season. *C* is for the cupcakes they ate to celebrate. You can follow him on Instagram @theotherjaybrazeau.

JANAY BROWN-WOOD is a former high school triathlete (volleyball, basketball, and swimming) who still loves being active. When she's not cheering for her daughter, Vivian, on the soccer field, she's writing books for children. She has more than twenty-five published books, including *Imani's Moon*, *The Simone Biles Little Golden Book Biography*, and the Love Puppies chapter book series. www.janaybrownwood.com

TANITA S. DAVIS grew up in suburban Northern California, proud to be the only girl on her seventh-grade intramural flag football team. Now over football and into stories, Tanita is the author of eleven books, including the NAACP Image Award–nominated and Coretta Scott King Award–winning novel *Mare's War*. www.tanitasdavis.com

MARIANA DOMINÉ grew up immersed in fútbol. Her father, who played in Argentina, brought that passion with him when immigrating to the United States. He coached Mariana and her sisters for most of their youth, and their family has built many memories around rooting for Lionel Messi. Her love for writing poetry runs as deep as her connection to the game. You can follow her on Instagram: @mariana.domine.poetry.

LEAH HENDERSON was a three-sport varsity athlete, and she has been playing soccer since she was big enough to dribble and slide tackle. As she got older, words became another love. She writes books for young readers including *The Courage of the Little Hummingbird*, *The Magic in Changing Your Stars*, and *Together We March*. www.leahhendersonbooks.com

NAAZ KHAN is a Muslim American educator who was born in India, grew up in California and Saudi Arabia, and has lived in Egypt, where Aprar's family is from. In addition to writing, she loves exploring meditative practices, including the martial arts of tai chi and kung fu. To learn about her debut picture book, *Room for Everyone*, and other upcoming books, visit www.naazkhan.org.

IRENE LATHAM writes from the Purple Horse Poetry Studio & Music Room, beside a mountain lake in Blount County, Alabama. While she's always preferred reading to participating in sports, she does find tremendous inspiration in athletes' stories. Her work with Charles Waters on this and other poetry anthologies brings much joy to her life. Read hundreds of Irene's poems for free at www.irenelatham.com.

NANCY TUPPER LING is a children's author, poet, bookseller, and librarian. She's also the anthologist, with coeditor June Cotner, of *Bless the Earth: A Collection of Poetry for Children to Celebrate and Care for Our World*, and the author of *Hearts in My Pocket*. Her favorite Olympic sport to watch nervously has always been freestyle skiing, and like Eileen, she's spent a lot of time with family in San Francisco. www.nancytupperling.com

GUADALUPE GARCÍA MCCALL grew up watching baseball with her papi in Eagle Pass, Texas. The Cincinnati Reds were her favorite team, and the World Series was a must-see in her family's home. She is the award-winning author of many books and poems for children and young adults, including *Under the Mesquite* and the national bestseller *Summer of the Mariposas*. www.ggmccall.com

EDNA CABCABIN MORAN loved the arts and sports as a kid. She played both American football and soccer. Her Polynesian dance background included Hawaiian hula, 'Ori Tahiti, and Samoan sasa. Edna's recent works as an author/illustrator include the Aesop Accolade title *Honu and Moa* and several poems in anthologies for young and middle-grade readers. www.kidlitedna.com

DARIUS PHELPS, PhD, is a poet, writer, and scholar whose work centers the liberatory possibilities of poetic inquiry, culturally responsive pedagogy, and critical literacy. A former elementary school teacher and now professor, he mentors preservice educators in reimagining classrooms as spaces of resistance, restoration, and radical love. He's an avid fan of basketball and soccer, and he can be found as @drdphelps on X and @dr.dphelps on Instagram.

GLENIS REDMOND, a former sprinter who ran the 100 meters and 200 meters and anchored the 4x400 relay, discovered her love for tennis as a young adult and now enjoys watching it on television. She is the first poet laureate of Greenville, South Carolina, and the author of seven poetry collections. www.Glenisredmond.com

KIM ROGERS is an award-winning author and a mom of boys who've played nearly every sport, including football. She writes poetry, short stories, and books for young readers. An enrolled member of Wichita and Affiliated Tribes, Kim lives with her family on her ancestral homelands in Oklahoma. www.kimrogerswriter.com

RENÉ SALDAÑA JR. played first and third bases for the Peñitas Raiders, batting .408 one year. Today, he drives his kids to their practices, games, and meets. In his spare time, he's a professor of literacy and the author of several books for young adults, among them *The Whole Sky Full of Stars and Eventually, Inevitably: My Writing Life in Verse*. He can be found on X as @ReneSaldanaJr.

LAURA SHOVAN grew up playing defense for her local soccer league. Among her award-winning children's books are *The Last Fifth Grade of Emerson Elementary*, *Takedown*, and *A Place at the Table*, written with Saadia Faruqi. Laura is a longtime poet-in-the-schools. She teaches adults at Vermont College of Fine Arts and mentors teen authors in the Navigating the Margins writing program. www.laurashovan.com

SARAH GRACE TUTTLE loves to swim, especially in quiet pools and ponds. When they were little, they liked to pretend they were a frog while swimming the breaststroke. They are the author of *Hidden City: Poems of Urban Wildlife* and other books for children. You can visit them online at www.sarahgracetuttle.com.

CHARLES WATERS grew up in the suburbs of Philadelphia, Pennsylvania. He played football in high school and used to be a sports-obsessed human. He's now coanthologist (with Irene Latham) of not only this book but others as well including *The Mistakes That Made Us: Confessions from Twenty Poets* and *If I Could Choose a Best Day: Poems of Possibility*. www.charleswaterspoetry.com

KAO KALIA YANG came to St. Paul, Minnesota, as a refugee child from the camps in Thailand. Yang is a proud member of the Hmong community, and like Suni Lee, she is from the East Side of St. Paul. She is an author of books for adults and children, among them *The Latehomecomer* and *A Map into the World*. Kalia writes about belonging, family, and love. www.kaokaliayang.com

ANITA YASUDA lives in the rolling hills of Ontario, hiking the trails and practicing yoga and meditation at her favorite lake. She is the author of many books for young people, including the picture book *Up, Up, Ever Up! Junko Tabei: A Life in the Mountains*. www.anitayasuda.com

SOURCE NOTES

endsheet “Sport has the . . . little else does.”: Nelson Mandela, “Nelson Mandela’s Iconic Speech—‘Sport Has the Power to Change the World’—Full Version,” YouTube video, 4:35, posted by Laureus, February 9, 2020, https://www.youtube.com/watch?v=y1-7w-bJCtY.

5 “I think if . . . so much easier.”: LeBron James, “Lebron James’ Advice to Young Kids and Basketball Players,” YouTube video, 0:37, posted by the Los Angeles Times, February 15, 2020, https://www.youtube.com/watch?v=hsBLIWHE4Gg.

7 “My parents sacrificed . . . me reach it.”: Sophia Wilson, “Sophia Smith: The Journey,” YouTube video, 1:53, posted by U.S. Soccer, October 26, 2022, https://www.youtube.com/watch?v=bxnKJwOPIP8.

9 “It’s life . . . not lose yourself.”: Keenan Allen, “NFL Films Presents: Keenan Allen’s Growth into a Top WR,” video, 1:10, Chargers, accessed April 9, 2025, https://www.chargers.com/video/nfl-films-presents-keenan-allen-s-growth-into-a-top-wr.

10 “Thinking back on . . . it was magical.”: Ronald Acuña Jr., “I Mean No Harm, I Swear,” The Players’ Tribune Signature, accessed April 9, 2025, https://projects.theplayerstribune.com/ronald-acuna-jr-atlanta-braves-mlb-baseball/p/1.

11 “I lived for . . . wanted to do.” Acuña.

13 “I gave it . . . all that matters.” Elizabeth Campbell, “Gymnast Suni Lee Says ‘I Gave It My All’ at 2024 Paris Olympics,” CBS News, August 5, 2024, https://www.cbsnews.com/news/suni-lee-2024-paris-olympics-gymnast-i-gave-it-my-all/.

15 “That day made . . . for the world.”: Sahil Gaswami, “‘Made Me Who I Am’: When Jalen Hurts Revealed Why He Smiles Thinking About Being Benched in National Championship Game,” sportskeeda, February 10, 2025, https://www.sportskeeda.com/college-football/made-i-am-when-jalen-hurts-revealed-smiles-thinking-benched-national-championship-game.

17 “I do hope . . . of any tunnel.”: Naomi Osaka, “Naomi Osaka: ‘It’s O.K. Not to Be O.K.’” *Time*, July 8, 2021, https://time.com/6077128/naomi-osaka-essay-tokyo-olympics/.

18 “Listen, one day . . . will be there.”: Jose de Jesus Ortiz, “As Dad Predicted, Nationals Phenom Soto Stars at World Series,” La Vida Baseball, October 23, 2019, https://www.lavidabaseball.com/game-1-world-series-juan-soto-father

19 “We were watching . . . just feels amazing.”: Juan Soto, “Juan Soto Joined Chris Rose and Kevin Millar on Intentional Talk and It Was . . . an Absolute Joy to Watch,” video, 2:10, Facebook, August 22, 2020, https://www.facebook.com/watch/?v=302120404226933.

21 “Hopefully I’m . . . time in Edmonton.”: Patrick Kearns, “How Connor McDavid Deals with Being the Youngest NHL Captain Ever,” *Rolling Stone*, October 17, 2016, https://www.rollingstone.com/culture/culture-sports/how-connor-mcdavid-deals-with-being-youngest-nhl-captain-ever-111766/.

23 “You have to . . . your own pace.”: A’ja Wilson, “Brute Strength,” The Players’ Tribune, March 24, 2018, https://www.theplayerstribune.com/articles/aja-wilson-south-carolina.

25 “I’m not just . . . that I do.” Matthew Allen, *Long Way Home: The Jessica Long Story*, Peacock, 4:48, NBC Sports Network, 2016.

27 “Life gets pretty . . . a lot easier.”: Ben Morse, “Jessica and Nelly Korda: The ‘Built-in Best Buddies’ Taking the Golfing World by Storm,” CNN Sports, December 29, 2021, https://www.cnn.com/2021/12/29/golf/jessica-nelly-korda-golf-spc-spt-intl/index.html.

27 “built-in best buddies”: Morse.

28 “They must let you fight!”: Aprar Hassan, interview with Naaz Khan, May 29, 2024.

28 "integration power": Tom Degun, "World Karate Federation Approves the Hijab for Competition," Inside the Games, January 3, 2013, https://www.insidethegames.biz/articles/1012301/world-karate-federation-approves-the-hijab-for-competition.

29 "If someone says . . . to become stronger.": Hassan, interview.

31 "Achieving the impossible . . . drawn me in.": Lorena Encabo and Andrew Binner, "Ailing (Eileen) Gu: 'Outside of Skiing I Am a Huge Nerd!'," Olympics.com, April 9, 2023, https://www.olympics.com/en/news/ailing-eileen-gu-studies-quantum-physics-huge-nerd-interview.

33 "I'm really burning . . . bright right now.": Baseline staff, "Quote of the Day: Coco Gauff Thanks Haters for Adding Gas to Her Fire "I'm Really Burning So Bright Right Now," Baseline, September 9, 2023, https://www.tennis.com/baseline/articles/quote-of-day-coco-gauff-thanks-haters-add-gas-fire-burning-bright-us-open.

35 "I feel like . . . our legacy strong.": Brady Aymond, "WWE's Roman Reigns Ready to Shine in Hometown," *Pensacola News Journal*, July 17, 2014, https://www.pnj.com/story/sports/2014/07/17/wwes-roman-reigns-ready-shine-hometown/12808857/.

36 "Well ahead of the game": Fabian Ardaya, "Mookie Betts Embraces His Voice in New Jackie Robinson-Themed Film: 'I Want to Affect Lives,'" *Athletic*, October 10, 2022, https://www.nytimes.com/athletic/3673598/2022/10/10/mookie-betts-jackie-robinson-documentary/.

37 "I don't want . . . more than that.": Brian Welk, "Mookie Betts Wants to 'Be Known as More Than an Athlete' with His Jackie Robinson Doc," *Wrap*, October 10, 2022, https://www.thewrap.com/mookie-betts-interview-jackie-robinson-documentary/.

38 "physical health is mental health": Simone Biles, quoted in Henry Austin, "What Are the 'Twisties?' Simone Biles Explains Gymnastics Struggle at Tokyo Olympics," NBC News, July 30, 2021, https://www.nbcnews.com/news/olympics/what-are-twisties-simone-biles-explains-gymnastics-struggle-tokyo-olympics-n1275460.

39 "[The bronze] means . . . through so much.": "Simone Biles on Her Beam Bronze: 'It Means More Than All the Golds,'" Olympics.com, August 3, 2021, https://olympics.com/en/news/gymnastics-simone-biles-beam-bronze-tokyo-social-media-reaction.

41 "Being a bit . . . it, particularly children.": César Chalala, "Messi's Goals Are Many and Life Saving," Pressenza, December 14, 2022, https://www.pressenza.com/2022/12/messis-goals-are-many-and-life-saving/.

43 "I want to . . . in this world.": Jade Scipioni, "Chiefs Quarterback Patrick Mahomes on Doing Business Deals: 'I Watch Mark Cuban a Lot,'" CNBC Make It, April 9, 2021, https://www.cnbc.com/2021/04/09/chiefs-patrick-mahomes-on-business-deals-i-watch-mark-cuban-a-lot.html.

ABOUT THE POETRY

The poems in this collection employ free verse or informal rhyme, with the exception of these:

"Ronald Acuña Jr. Dreams of a Ringing Single" by René Saldaña Jr., which is a golden shovel poem. In this form, a quote is selected, and in the new poem the words that make up the quote are placed in order at the end of each line.

"Simone Biles Trounces the Twisties" by Tanita S. Davis, which is a pantoum. This form consists of a series of quatrains, where the second and fourth lines of each stanza are repeated as the first and third lines of the next stanza. This pattern continues throughout the poem, with the final stanza incorporating lines from the first stanza.

ACKNOWLEDGMENTS

The anthologists would like to thank the following:

The entire bookmaking team at Lerner Publishing Group, especially Andy Cummings for revitalizing this project during a lovely conversation; Adam Lerner for his passion for sports and for believing in this book; Kimberly Morales for her book designing talents; Danielle Carnito for her artistic magic; Delores Barton for her copyediting skills; Jon Fishman for helping us home in on which athletes to highlight; Lucien Brinkley for his expertise in matching photographs with poems; and last but never least, the incomparable Carol Hinz for her kindness and keen editorial judgment. #proudtobealerner

Our kidlit community, especially Bill Johnson for being a friend, inspiration, and all-around class act, and Yuko Shimizu for writer connections and assistance.

Rosemary Stimola, our literary agent, and everyone at Stimola Literary Studio.

The athletes for inspiring us. The poets for sharing their artistry.

And YOU dear reader. May the poems inspired by the lives of these athletes help guide you on your journey.

PHOTO ACKNOWLEDGMENTS

Image credits: AP Photo/David Zalubowski, p. 5; Brad Smith/ISI/Getty Images, p. 7; AP Photo/Kelvin Kuo, p. 9; AP Photo/John Minchillo, p. 11; Ezra Shaw/Getty Images, p. 13; Robin Alam/Icon Sportswire via Getty Images, p. 15; Ciol/Abaca/Sipa USA via AP Images, p. 17; Alex Trautwig/MLB Photos via Getty Images, p. 19; Thearon W. Henderson/Getty Images, p. 21; Richard W. Rodriguez/Fort Worth Star-Telegram/Tribune News Service via Getty Images, p. 23; Adam Pretty/Getty Images, p. 25; David Becker/Getty Images, p. 27; Courtesy of Aprar Hassan, p. 29; AP Photo/Gregory Bull, p. 31; Fred Mullane/ISI Photos/Getty Images, p. 33; WWE/Getty Images, p. 35; Matt Dirksen/Getty Images, p. 37; Laurence Griffiths/Getty Images, p. 39; Julian Finney/Getty Images, p. 41; Ryan Kang/Getty Images, p. 43. Design elements: robbylokamp/Shutterstock; suns07butterfly/Shutterstock.

Author photo credits: Cheryl Lowe (Jamie Adoff); Richard Louissant (Lacresha Berry); Heather MacLeod (Jay Brazeau); Mickaela Colvin Photography (JaNay Brown-Wood); David T. Macknet (Tanita S. Davis); Green Pearl Photography (Mariana Dominé); Courtesy of Leah Henderson; Nadia El-Dasher (Naaz Khan); Eric Latham (Irene Latham); Stacy Murphy Photography (Nancy Tupper Ling); Michael Mercado Smith (Guadalupe García McCall); Lisa Keating (Edna Cabcabin Moran); Courtesy of Darius Phelps; Amber McDowell Photography (Glenis Redmond); Prints Charming (Kim Rogers); Brad Tollefson (René Saldaña Jr.); Linda Joy Burke (Laura Shovan); Xavid Pretzer (Sarah Grace Tuttle); C. Dyer Photography (Charles Waters); Shee Yang (Kao Kalia Yang); Reflections by Patty (Anita Yasuda).

Cover: AP Photo/Chris Szagola; AP Photo/Charlie Riedel; Cooper Neill via AP; Peter Joneleit/Icon Sportswire via AP Images; AP Photo/John Raoux.